Chamuco
& Other Minimalist Writings

Armando Lopez

Copyright © 2017 by Armando Lopez
Chamuco & Other Minimalist Writings

All rights reserved, including the reproduction
in whole or in part in any form
without the written consent of the author.

ISBN 978-0-9971257-0-2

Excerpt from "*Arts Poetica*" by Jackson Wheeler published in
Was I Asleep: New and Selected Poems, © 2017.
Reprinted by permission of the Jackson Wheeler Trust.

Book Design and Illustrations by David Reeser and Amy Schneider

BLUE JAY INK

Published in the United States
by Blue Jay Ink,
451 A East Ojai Avenue
Ojai California 93023

bluejayink.com

Any resemblance to people living or dead is purely coincidental.

DEDICATION

To my wife Luly and my daughters Xilomen, Angelica and Ixchel for their love and support.

To my parents Antonio and Maria and my grandmothers Josefa and Zeferina.

FOREWARD

These charming, deceptively simple cameos might be lit by candlelight. By turns comic and tender, here are some of life's corners and cul-de-sacs rendered by a minimalist master.   –Aram Saroyan

"Words bear witness."

Jackson Wheeler

Chamuco & Other Writings
Armando Lopez

About Me	11
Name	13
Chamuco	15
No English	17
Confusion	19
Pepa	21
Windy Day	23
A Sign	25
Bacon and Eggs	27
My People	29
First Jump	31
My Moment	33
Soft Air	35
Peddler	37
Empty Store	39
Faucet	41
Keynote	43
First Time	45
Unfriendly	47
One Night	49
Menu	51
Amused	53
Waiting	55
Doña	57
The Candle	59
Click	61
Memory	63
Inevitable	65
Gates	67
Maybe	69

A PEEK INTO MY MINIMALIST LIFE

I was born on December 25, 1945 in Oxnard, California in a converted garage on the alley behind C Street and across the street from Driffill School.

I started kindergarten there at four years old and didn't speak a word of English. There was another little boy there named Zeke Ruelas who didn't speak English either.

We became best friends on that first day and have remained friends. We picked up English rather quickly.

As a child, I had what I needed, but nothing more.

My father built us a two-bedroom, one bath house.

Early on, I felt uncomfortable accumulating things. Smaller was always preferable to bigger and less to more.

Well, that's enough about me. Hope you enjoy my minimalist writings.

NAME

The doctor arrives at the house,
somewhat intoxicated.

He got here just in time to cut the cord and tie it off.

"Got anything to drink?" he asks my father.

My father had been drinking since before midnight.

The doctor says that because of the holiday,
my name should be Salvador.

My father doesn't like the name and wants to name me Antonio.

They begin to argue as drunks do.

The doctor stands up and storms out of the house.

My birth certificate arrives in our mailbox.

My name is Salvador.

CHAMUCO

My brother left when he was four.

I was three.

Soon after, his dog, Chamuco, left home.

Some time later, Chamuco returned.

We were very happy to see him.

He walked through the house, room by room.

Chamuco left again.

NO ENGLISH

My mother drops me off at school.

It's my first day of kindergarten.

I don't speak English.

My teacher doesn't speak Spanish.

I feel alone and I need to pee.

She takes my hand.

No English needed.

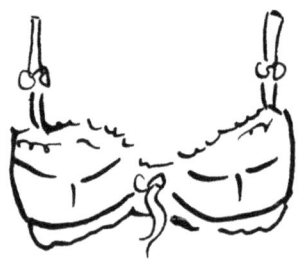

CONFUSION

I'm in the 7th grade.

Home from school.

Anxious to change clothes.

Football game in the street.

Live-in housekeeper yells from her bedroom.

"You can't leave yet!"

"But the guys are waiting!" I shout back.

"Come into my bedroom."

In a rush, I obey and find her standing next to her bed.

She opens her mouth to speak.

"Do you like my new underwear?"

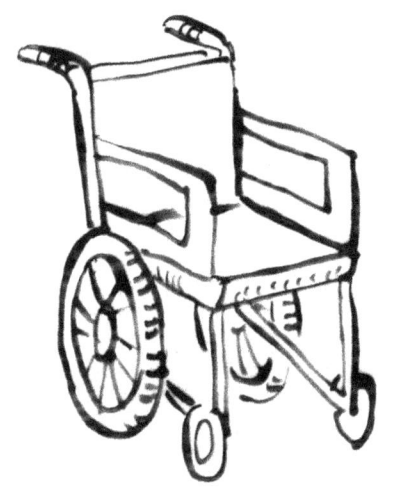

PEPA

I loved my grandmother.

She was very old.

I was very young.

She was bedridden and lived with my uncle.

We went to see her.

Before returning home, I went to kiss her.

Crying she said, "I won't see you again."

She was right.

WINDY DAY

It's an exciting day.

Very windy and hot!

I look out the window.

They're coming down the street!

My excitement is growing!

They're getting closer!

I make my move!

I run out to the middle of the street and lie down.

The first tumbleweed rolls over me!

A SIGN

Sitting in class, I wonder if the devil exists.

I decide to find out.

First stop, the local Catholic Church.

"Bless me, Father. My last confession…"

Next, I'm standing in a large, dark, windowless warehouse.

I clear my throat.

"If you exist, give me a sign."

My nose begins to itch!

BACON AND EGGS

Can I ask you a question?

Sure.

What do you guys eat for breakfast?

What do you mean *you guys*?

Spanish people.

We aren't Spanish.

You know what I mean!

Well, sometimes, we have cereal, bacon and eggs, hot cakes, or even French toast.

Wow, that's just like us!

Except our eggs come from Mexican chickens.

MY PEOPLE

I'm in my student government meeting.

Subject is the Governor's Conference on Juvenile Delinquency.

I'm elected to represent our high school.

A beautiful cheerleader comes up.

"Glad you're representing our high school," she says.

"Your people need it."

FIRST JUMP

This is my first qualifying parachute jump.

I'm more than nervous standing on the runway waiting to board.

The sergeant stands in front of the guy next to me, checks his equipment, and steps back.

He yells over the blast of the C-130.

"What are you?"

The future paratrooper, as rehearsed, screams back, "Airborne, Sergeant!"

It's now my turn.

He checks my equipment, steps back and yells, "What are you?"

"Mexican American, Sergeant."

MY MOMENT

I sit next to her.

I don't know how to tell her that there can never be anyone else.

Suddenly she turns,

"Excuse me, sir, this is my stop."

SOFT AIR

It has me in a trance,

That flame that dances to the music of love,

That flame that dances in her image.

The image moves towards me as warm, soft air.

I reach out and touch her.

PEDDLER

I'm a peddler!

Wanna buy?

I'm a peddler!

Come on by!

That's my game!

What's your name?

I'm a peddler!

Wanna buy?

EMPTY STORE

The old man sweeps.

He's not sure why.

Every stroke of the broom leaves more than it sweeps up.

Another empty store, another empty day.

The phone rings!

Wrong number.

FAUCET

"My ironing board isn't closing properly.

Will you come over and take a look?"

Sure.

I take my cousin.

He's good with tools.

"My curtains fell..."

I take my cousin.

He's good with tools.

"My faucet is leaking ..."

Come alone."

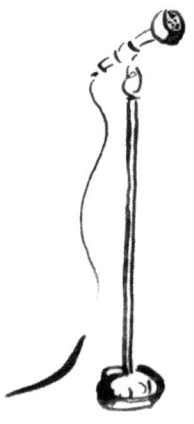

KEYNOTE

I just took my seat.

It's a tablecloth evening.

Three-piece suits,

Dust face matrons.

Everyone sitting where they've sat before.

Keynote, old note, sorrowful tune.

It all started with howling at the moon.

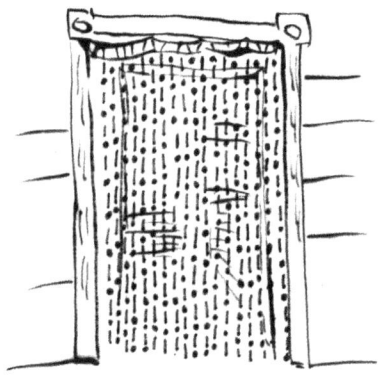

FIRST TIME

You look scared.

I am.

Is this your first time?

Yes.

Where you from?

Small village in the Central Valley.

If you want, we can just talk.

But I have to give him the money.

Let's just talk.

UNFRIENDLY

"That guy over there keeps looking at you," he says.

I turn around.

The guy gives me an unfriendly look.

I excuse myself to go to the restroom.

I'm standing at the urinal.

The door opens.

It's him.

I'm drying my hands when he walks up.

"I'm going to kick your ass!" he says.

I respond in the only way I know how:

"Call the office and make an appointment!"

ONE NIGHT

Beautiful voice.

I send her a drink.

Beautiful face.

She comes to my table.

Beautiful laugh.

She spends the night.

What was her name?

MENU

Would you like soup or salad with that?

What soups do you have?

Clam chowder, chicken with rice, and vegetable.

And salads?

Garden and Caesar.

What kind of dressing do you have?

Ranch, thousand island, Italian, and blue cheese.

Bring me a cheeseburger with fries!

AMUSED

I'm listening to a panel of literature professors.

They are discussing an author's latest book.

"There's no way the author meant that!"

"It should be obvious to you."

"What's obvious is that you missed the whole point of the novel."

Sitting in the back, I glance over.

The author is sitting there with an amused look.

WAITING

I have been at my father's bedside for hours.

His breathing is labored.

My father was there when I took my first breath.

I am determined to see him take his last.

His chest heaves gently up and down, but the sound it makes tells me not to leave his side.

The nurse stands in front of me and leans over to check on him.

She runs out of the room.

His chest is still.

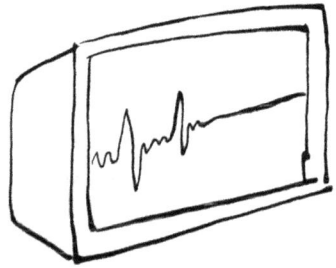

DOÑA

"Is there any hope?"

"None."

"Is she able to hear me?"

"No."

I whisper in her ear anyway.

"Mom, thank you for always loving and caring for us.

I want you to let go now.

Dad's waiting for you."

I look up at the nurse and nod.

Countdown .....

Flatline.

THE CANDLE

"She hasn't called back."

Patience, the candle is still burning.

"She didn't call. Still think she'll call?"

Yes, the candle is still burning.

"I left another message!"

Don't worry. The candle is still burning.

"I can't sleep. This waiting is killing me."

Relax. The candle is still burning.

Sudden gust of wind.

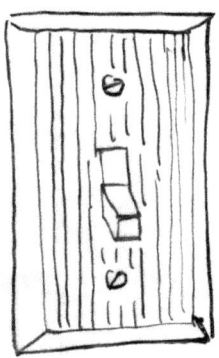

CLICK

I just bought this great device.

Click, the lights go off.

Click, the alarm is set.

Click, the coffee is brewing.

Click, my car starts.

Click, the garage door closes.

Home from work.

Dead battery.

I'm screwed.

MEMORY

I swear this was my father's room.

The nightstand, the TV set...

The bathroom,

The tree outside the window.

Nurse, where's my dinner?!

INEVITABLE

They say death is inevitable.

Ashes to ashes and dust to dust.

Make mine sawdust.

GATES

Have you been waiting a long time?

Don't remember. Calendars and clocks aren't allowed.

Any idea when we will be allowed inside?

We were told our time will come.

Have you seen him?

No.

Has anyone?

I don't think so.

Wonder what it's like inside...

No one knows.

...Are those real pearls on the gates?

MAYBE

I'm dead; so if you're reading this, you're not.

To my friends,

Thank you.

To my enemies,

Congratulations.

Don't donate to my causes.

There are too many.

Just one request:

Plant a tree in a public space.

No bronze plaque.

Just a tree.

See you ... maybe.

ACKNOWLEDGEMENTS

I want to express my appreciation to all those who made this book possible. My appreciation extends to those who have touched my life along the way.

There are some I would like to mention by name: Luther Wallace, who sparked my interest in writing; Aram Saroyan, friend and advisor; Fermin Herrera, my compadre, for his thoughts over the years; Heidi Bradbury, who inspired me to finally sit down and write; Suzanne Bellah, for her help and enthusiasm; wife Luly for her feedback; daughter Ixchel, my counselor and talented editor; to my assistant Leticia Bautista, for your help with the final copy, Marcela Franco for your support, and Amy Schneider and Dave Reeser, my publishers at Blue Jay Ink for your advice and support.

ABOUT THE AUTHOR

Armando Lopez was born and raised in Oxnard, California, a coastal city 60 miles north of Los Angeles. He graduated from California State University, Northridge and has a California Community College Teaching Credential. He has taught courses in literature and history at Moorpark and Oxnard Colleges.

In his early years he worked as a support services counselor for farmworkers in basic education programs and on-the-job training programs for low income participants.

Today he's in business and still makes Oxnard his home.

www.ingramcontent.com/pod-product-compliance
Lightning Source LLC
LaVergne TN
LVHW041550070426
835507LV00011B/1022